Jefferson, Reagan and a new Conservatism for 2014

Can Conservatives Still Save America?

Chris Schnupp

DEDICATION

To my loving wife and family

CONTENTS

INTRODUCTION

Jefferson delivered his first inaugural address to a crowded Senate chamber on March 4th, 1801. It was the first time since the writing of the Constitution that a different party was in power. Jefferson's election was heavily contested by the Federalists, and a significant amount of fear mongering over his Republican values caused many Americans to worry about the security of a new government. When Jefferson spoke, it was by no means a lengthy speech, but he took the opportunity to clearly establish his beliefs on government and personal freedom. Nearly 176 years later, Ronald Reagan, recently defeated in a Republican primary spoke at CPAC. Like Jefferson he delivered a short, but powerful speech outlining the role of government, the value of conservatism and personal choice. Analyzing both speeches creates questions about the role of Conservatism in America Today.

1 JEFFERSON

An enduring legend of the Jefferson inauguration was the essential metaphor for Jeffersonian Republicanism. Historian Joseph J. Ellis has shed some light onto the myth of the Jefferson inauguration and what had been portrayed as a simple ride into town on horseback, and walking by himself into the Senate to speak was more myth than reality. Although Jefferson did have a parade, it was small in comparison to Washington and Adams. He did not use the same large diplomat style carriage that his predecessors used, instead he walked. Jefferson was staying at a boardinghouse that was less than a few blocks from the Capitol Building. He was escorted by militia from the moment he left the boardinghouse to his entrance into the Senate. Rather than speaking to a small room of people, it is estimated that the Senate was packed with over 1,000 people. While true no one could hear the speech due to his mumbling, or low voice, the speech had been printed previously (1998). However the myth endures to some degree because of the content of the speech itself, and Jefferson's strong opinions on how Government should act.

Jefferson, as writer of the Declaration of Independence, borrowed heavily from principles of John Locke used in his Two Treatises of Government. While Locke would argue for a contract between a monarch and his or her people, Jefferson noticed the despotic tendencies of a monarch may not allow for a simple contract to exist. It was probably said best by Samuel Adams' in a 1776 speech at the State House in Philadelphia; he remarked that "the property, lives and religion of millions...are not bound to be victims to cruel and unforgiving despotism." The document itself served the purpose of furnishing Britain with a list of complaints citing instances where there had been a violation of political, economic or social rights. Taking the influence from Locke and the common belief shared with Adams Jefferson wrote that "all men are created equal, and they are endowed by their creator with certain unalienable Rights, chief among them Life, Liberty and the Pursuit of Happiness. That to secure these rights, Governments are instituted among men..."

Jefferson was therefore rightly disappointed with both Washington and Adams with the manner in which government was progressing. The government was taking on a greater role than the Declaration had allowed. Jefferson referred to his own election as a revolution, and a return to the "spirit" of 76. The Federalists were concerned that austerity minded Jefferson would simply throw out the system of government as outlined by the Constitution. Ardent and loyal Federalists spent weeks holding up the Jefferson nomination on a voting technicality. On the opposite side of the argument were the Republicans who looked forward to returning the Government to its proper place.

The speech carefully outlines the Jeffersonian belief in government. The first quality Jefferson mentions is freedom to use our own faculties. To Jefferson the freedom of expression was incredibly important. It was Jefferson who had written the Declaration after all, he understood the right to question government, and to be able to think for him, rather than be dictated to by an over-reaching government.

Secondly Jefferson mentions economy. The free-market system and the ability to develop products was not how colonial markets were run. A colonial power would dictate production, including what to produce and at what price. Additionally Britain set tariff and tax rates on goods, in some cases crippling local small businesses.

Jefferson next mentions that the government should not exist based off of birthright but from electing fellow citizens based on their actions and understanding of the world. Jefferson firmly believed that a class system existed, however it was a class based off of education. Those that sought out and excelled in education should, in Jefferson's mind, make excellent candidates for government. He argued for a two tier educational system in which the best and the brightest would seek out a college education, while the remainder of the population would be encouraged towards other pursuits. Although Jefferson was not successful, he did provide a model for the elementary public school system.

Religion was next on the inaugural list, where he

mentions that religion, while practiced differently, provides

people with values and beliefs, chief among them:

"...honesty, truth, temperance, gratitude, and the love of

man; acknowledging and adoring an overruling

Providence." To the founders it did not matter what religion

a person practiced. They did not feel it was within the scope

of government to determine what god or gods you should

pray to, and in fact if no god was your choice. John Adams

was born a 40 years after and 30 miles from the Salem Witch

Trials. Most founding fathers were aware of the power that

King Henry VIII had assumed in making himself the head of

the church and state. They feared what despotism could be

created in the name of religion, much like that, which

resulted in the Spanish Inquisition with the persecution of

Jews. At no time did the founding fathers envision a world

without religion, of those at the constitutional convention, 28

were Episcopalian, eight Presbyterian, seven

Congregationalists, and two each were Catholic, Lutheran,

Dutch Reform and Methodist. Thomas Paine was likely a Deists, and it has been argued that Jefferson, Adams, Washington, Madison, Hamilton and Morris were theistic rationalists (Lambert, 2003). This again refers to the Declaration's claim that all were "endowed by their creator with certain unalienable Rights," and it was simply the government's job to protect those rights.

For effect, Jefferson's last item on the list was a "wise and frugal government." While people in their daily lives had personal choice in thought, work, and religion, to Jefferson, the most important choice was actually out of the hands of the individual. While the citizenry would empower government, it was up to the government to act appropriately on their behalf. From the moment that the Constitution was being constructed, Jefferson was leery of the powers that were given to various branches. As Samuel Adams had stated: a government, despotic in nature, could simply trample the rights of its subjects without any recourse. If the framers of the Constitution could devise a plan that would have protected the rights of individuals, by ensuring that the government existed simply as a method of ensuring that the rights of the citizens could not be taken away arbitrarily, then Jefferson may have been more likely to fully support a Federalist point of view. Assigned to Paris for much of the convention, James Madison served as Jefferson's voice, although, by the end, Madison conceded the role of the executive; however he proposed a series of amendments to ensure that rights were protected.

The Bill of Rights that Madison proposed was extensive, including 39 amendments initially. Alexander Hamilton seemed to take a Jeffersonian approach to the Bill of Rights and voiced a concern in 1788 that including a Bill of Rights to the Constitution may in fact give those who seek to be despotic a means of pointing to the rights, and stating that as written these are the only rights of the citizenry. Even a reserved powers clause in the 10th Amendment was not any solace to Hamilton, as he felt

> I go further, and affirm that bills of rights, in the sense and to the extent in which they are contended for, are not only unnecessary in the proposed Constitution, but would even be dangerous. They would contain various exceptions to powers not granted; and, on this very account, would afford a colorable pretext to claim more than were granted. For why declare that things shall not be done which there is no power to do? Why, for instance, should it be said that the liberty of the press shall not be restrained, when no power is given by which restrictions may be imposed? I will not contend that such a provision would confer a regulating power; but it is evident that it would furnish, to men disposed to usurp, a plausible pretense for claiming that power.

Without many options, Jefferson inherited the government that Alexander Hamilton and George Washington sought. Rather than dismantle the government, Jefferson made the following promises: the government will create laws to prevent people from injuring one another.

People should be free to pursue business and to improve themselves as they saw fit. Most important of all that the government would not "take from the mouth of labor the bread it has earned." Jefferson mentioned in a later paragraph that the labor should be lightly burdened. Jefferson felt that the government should not spend so much money that it felt necessary to heavily tax the working public. On a national scale, Jefferson promised that he would not engage in foreign alliances, and that the government should act as a support for the states, as they are "the most competent administrators of our domestic concerns." Jefferson argued for a militia that should act in emergencies until the Regulars could be called into act. He wanted an honest repayment of the national debt, and to protect those rights enumerated in the first amendment.

Although Jeffersonian Republicanism would only last until 1825, with one speech, Jefferson was able to clearly identify what the intention of the Declaration of Independence was, as well as establish the role for the government under the Constitution. The first inaugural speech is the foundation of core Conservative values and beliefs that still exist today.

2 REAGAN

When Ronald Reagan, actor, turned politician spoke at the CPAC conference in 1977 he had just lost a primary race to Gerald Ford. Ford in turn was handily beaten at the ballot box by Democrat Jimmy Carter. Reagan felt that neither party was offering solutions that would deal with the major issues facing America. Ford primary win was a clear indication that the party system was still firmly in place, and that reliance on party mantras may not fix all of the problems facing America. In the years leading up the 1976 election, reliance on foreign energy led to an oil crisis in 1973, as well playing a role in the stock market crash in 1973-

74. Terrorism which would come to dominate headlines in the 1980's was first seen on American soil in 1975. A bomb set off in New York City killed four and injured sixty; this was shortly after the 1972 televised terrorist attack on the Munich Olympics. The incredible rise to power of Brezhnev in the Soviet Union, where since 1968, the Soviets invaded Czechoslovakia, fought the Chinese in a border war, and signed a treaty with the US to ensure equality in nuclear weaponry. Worst of all neither party had been able to roll back the socialist expansion of government under Franklin Roosevelt.

Realizing that the party was straying from its mission, Reagan took the opportunity at CPAC to directly appeal to all Conservatives, regardless of party to join together to stop the radicalized progressives from driving America over an economic and social cliff. To address these issues Reagan highlighted   areas   of   concern   that   should   unite

Conservatives: economy, government spending, education, government overreach, common sense and common decency.

For Reagan it was most important to establish that the ideals put forth by Jefferson still existed, although they were spread out across two parties. Quoting a 1975 Harris poll, that identified 31% of the population as Conservative, 41% moderate and 18% Liberal, Reagan noted that a majority of Americans actually consider themselves Conservative. He did though understand that there was a deep division between those that were socially conservative and those that were economically conservative.

Reagan strongly believed that being socially and economically conservative was not mutually exclusive goals, and that the ideology of a person identifying themselves as Conservative is actually a core set of similar values and beliefs. Yet Conservatives were being overshadowed by a

Republican party that had become associated with big business, stigmatized with a corrupt Nixon presidency, all which made the party look secretive and exclusionary.

Knowing that winning an election meant compromising with Democrats, Reagan began his speech, not touting any of the major platforms he sought in 1980 election, rather he spent time identifying the similar interests of the two groups of Conservatives. He even proposed a New Republican party, should that be necessary, to ensure that a conservative majority, would be properly represented in government. The very first political point that Reagan makes about Conservatism is that the central ideal of the ideology is common sense. Reagan points out that certain ideologies like Marxist-Leninist theory require abstraction that does not work in the real world whereas Jeffersonian Republicanism has proven to work. Reagan then continues to point out through examples some of the key elements of

Conservatism: balanced budget, local government control on domestic issues, as well as common sense, common decency and religion. The manner of which Reagan approaches each of these issues is by stating that an understanding of modern government is to believe in Conservatism and to realize through concrete examples that socialism does not work. It was close to the idea that John Adams espoused: "Facts are stubborn things; and whatever may be our wishes, our inclinations, or the dictates of our passions, they cannot alter the state of facts and evidence." To Reagan and likewise to Conservatives the knowledge that socialism does not work, regardless of what the wishes of politicians might be, is fact, supported by years of evidence.

Unlike Jefferson, Reagan had to make a direct appeal to the voters who were disinterested or distrustful of the government. The Republican Party, which had sought to establish equality for all had led the charge to free the slaves, and elected a Republican president in Abraham Lincoln who traded his life to ensure that slavery would no longer exist as an institution, not just as a military action, but through the passage of the 13th Amendment, which outlawed slavery. Theodore Roosevelt during his presidency fought against big-business and established the National Parks Service. When it came time to review a bill on granting women the right to vote, Republicans in the house voted 81-34 in favor of the bill. Their Democratic counterparts had voted 170-85 against the legislation. It was not until Franklin Roosevelt that the Republican Party was no longer associated with the protection of the public's freedoms. Due to the failings of Republican Herbert Hoover, whether accurate or not, Franklin Roosevelt was initially given carte blanche to attempt to pull the United States out of a crippling depression. The extent to which Franklin used the government was essentially to control businesses and to use the treasury to redistribute wealth. A tax burden was placed on the worker in order to pay for programs that had no means of becoming self-sustaining. Margaret Thatcher is attributed as saying that "Socialism is great, until you run out of other people's money."

The socialist tendency of the Democratic Party also led to the Lyndon Johnson "Great Society" that further burdened a system with non-self-sustaining programs. Reagan commented that the Great Society was great only in cost, size and power. To that end, he argued that the attempt of social engineering by the government had failed, and it was time to move towards more economically sound policies.

The Republicans in reaction to Roosevelt and Johnson embraced the economic conservatism that alienated the poor, minority and social conservative. For Reagan, he was fighting a stigma that the Republican Party, former champion of rights no longer cared about people, and was only in existence for businesses that funded them. His appeal was to the Democratic Conservatives, specifically those who were ignored in the New Deal and Great Society. Reagan understood that the actual teaching of values, morals, and beliefs occurs within the family. Naturally he was concerned with government programs that sought to usurp the family, and downplay the importance of family in creating a stable society. With this in mind Reagan sought out the minority vote with the belief that a society functions better when family values, jobs and freedom are the goals of all citizens. Reagan promised a better and brighter future for minorities through education, jobs and hopefully a refocus on the importance of family.

The global concern of freedom is where Reagan and Jefferson begin to separate in their beliefs. While Jefferson argued that foreign alliances would consistently require

American forces to be shipped abroad, Reagan realized that the advent of long range ICBM, long range aircraft and the problems posed by nuclear weapons meant that the United States may no longer be able to turn away from world politics. Reagan referred to the Freedom House map, which separates countries into three categories: free, somewhat free, not free. Reagan talked of those areas such as Russia, Asia, Africa and the Middle East where no freedoms exist. However, Reagan did not argue for domination of the world by the United States. He argued instead for truth, peace, and a re-examination of the policies that America had developed towards these counties in the years following World War II. Reagan stated the importance of maintaining a powerful military, not for tyrannical purposes, but for deterrence. To this end, he wanted the CIA to stop being demonized, and for citizens to understand and take an interest in National Security.

What Reagan realized was how a progressive liberal economic and social agenda was about to cause a general crisis in America. By July of 1979, Carter, without real solutions, listed the magnitude of American problems in what has become known as the "Crisis in Confidence Speech." There he described the ongoing energy crisis, and the gasoline shortage which paralyzed a nation. He went on to discuss a lack of respect for schools and religion, and an overall distrust of government. The Iran Hostage crisis had not yet occurred, but would come to signify Carter's ineptitude in office. The fear that a liberal ideology, empowered with running the country, would result in chaos both socially and economically was realized. Reagan's plan as described at CPAC resulted in a united Conservative approach, and as a result he held a mandate of 50.1% of the popular vote and a landslide 90.9% of the electoral vote in the 1980 Presidential Election (Leip, 2012).

3 SINCE REAGAN

The US GDP had the highest percentage of recent growth under Reagan at roughly eight percent. During the 1990's the GDP had almost a zero percent growth until the Gingrich "Contract with America" which restored growth to about five percent. This lasted until 2001 when there was a slight drop and 2008 when there was a negative percentage growth. Currently GDP growth sits at 1.9% and is declining again (World Bank, 2014). Private businesses as of the end of 2013 have had the smallest growth rate (5.4%) since the 2009 collapse. This marks a large drop in growth since 2011 when the growth rate was 9.6%. Of those companies that are considered to be small, those with under $10 million in sales saw their growth rate drop from eight percent to an average of four percent. Large manufacturers went from double digits to 3.2% (Biery, 2014). Sound fiscal policy with the Gingrich-led Congress was replaced by large governmental agencies reminiscent of the Great Society. In further pursuit of this socialist agenda, poor economic policies and high debt followed. The government has expanded the national debt from around $3 trillion when Reagan left office, to a staggering $17 trillion in October of 2013.

Prior to Reagan taking office, government spending on entitlement programs was at an all-time high of 30% of the GDP. He was able to institute welfare reform and sound fiscal policies that brought the percentage under the 30% mark. After Reagan left office, the spending increased again at an exponential rate, reaching 47% in 2010 (Chantrill, 2014).

During the transition from Carter to Reagan, participation in the food stamp program reached 22 million. By the end of the Reagan presidency the number had been reduced to 18 million. As of 2013, 47 million people are on food stamps, with the total cost near $80 million (USDA, 2014). Today the workforce participation rate has matched a 1978 low point of 62.8 percent (Stilwell, 2014).

Jefferson argued for a two tier educational system in which the best and the brightest would seek out a college education, while the remainder of the population would be encouraged towards other pursuits. Reagan also felt education was vitally important, as only 11% of students in the 1980's were heading towards a college education. However the heeding of Jefferson was not taken into consideration, as the market for college education exploded. Careers that had never required advanced degrees before suddenly demanded higher education. The New York City

Police Department requires 60 college credits in order to be eligible for the examination. The average cost of an associate degree at a community college in New York is $9,000. The base pay for an NYPD recruit is $41,975. Paying off college on a recruit's salary, combined with the costs of equipment, housing and food is not reasonable. Worse, the requirement for credit is not actually related to learning about policing, criminal justice, public administration or law, the credits do not have to be towards any particular degree. Part of this drive towards education has actually had a negative effect on the economy in two ways. First, debt has increased drastically. Although more students are going to college now, 71% of college graduates leave school in debt. The debt total for students is near $1 trillion. Nearly seven million students are at least 270 days late on their debt repayment (Bidwell, 2013). Secondly once in college, students are seeking out those jobs that will pay back the cost of education. Mike Rowe, who has made a career of tracking professions that would be considered blue-collar, or trade, has penned an open letter that points out that students are not entering the trades anymore, and as a result, the demand for a competent workforce outpaces availability (Ritz, 2013). In many ways, the "Dirty Jobs" celebrity is correct. Teaching jobs, for which there were once in high demand, now has a slower than average growth rate of 6% for high school teachers, many schools require the teacher to have a master's degree. Lawyers, required to have a doctorate only have a 10% growth rate.

Although the second tier of Jefferson's plan did not take hold, the lower tier became the model for the elementary public school system. Starting in 1821 the idea of a secondary school took hold in the northeast, and by 1870 most states had free basic education. Jefferson and Reagan agreed that the school system remained the domain of the States, though there was concern of the lack of progress of

American students. According to Newt Gingrich the reason is that the American educational system teaches as if it was still 1890. What we have learned since that time is that students are not one size fits all. However, education was co-opted by the government when the Common Core and No Child Left Behind were enacted as part of legislation. Through this legislation, the ability for instructors to individualize education has been removed and instead, laws have established a standardization system that strips away the ability for students to achieve and excel in their studies. Not only are the studies standardized, but the government also introduced a penalization system for those students and schools that do not meet the standard. Instead of providing advanced and challenging education to ensure that the brightest of students excelled and became leaders within America, the best students become bored as the class attempts to have the lowest performing students meet the minimum standards.

In addition to the questionable standards system, the progressive movement (which charged that education should teach the whole child, mentally, physically, emotionally and in subject content) has instead radicalized our educational system. Core subject areas including history and the arts have been casually thrust aside to focus on math and literacy. Even in those classes where the material is still somewhat content based the focus has been taking away from learning and instead placed unreasonable demands on instructors and students to pass the standardized test. Worse the study of American history for those taking AP courses has become so radicalized that founding fathers, the Constitution and much of the formation of America has been left out of the curriculum (Berry, 2014). Teachers have abandoned content teaching for test taking strategies. Recess no longer exists in favor of increased studies and remediation.

Reagan was a strong proponent of keeping a large military force as a show of strength. Military spending dropped from about $550 million in 1988 to just under $400 million in 1999, only to have the worst terror attack on American soil since Pearl Harbor. Since then spending rose to nearly $800 million but has sharply declined since 2010 and was at nearly $600 million in 2013. The Freedom House map that Reagan referred to in 1977 remains largely unchanged with 40% of the world free, 25% partially free and 35% not free. Those areas that were of particular concern to Reagan: Russia, Africa, Middle East, Asia remain unfree today, and are still the source of major concern. The nations in the Middle East have been a source of constant trouble for the United States due to careless, almost criminal land division by the British and French following World War. The two victorious nations paid little respect to religion, sectional difference and prior conflict, and created conglomerated nations based off of lines they drew onto a map. America has

now been draw into the three distinct wars within the region

requiring heavy military influence, and countless smaller

skirmishes that drain our military and budget as the threat

of terrorism increases.

In regards to civil liberties, there have been some major

regressions since Reagan. A Gallup poll in 2011 showed that

49% of Americans believed that the federal government

poses an immediate threat to individual's rights and

freedoms (Turley, 2011). Jefferson stated in 1819:

> Of liberty I would say that, in the whole
> plenitude of its extent, it is unobstructed
> action according to our will. But rightful
> liberty is unobstructed action according to our
> will within limits drawn around us by the
> equal rights of others.

While often thought to be a quote related to the Revolution,

Benjamin Franklin in his Poor Richards Almanac wrote: "Sell

not virtue to purchase wealth, nor Liberty to purchase

power." What both Jefferson and Franklin realized is that liberty is and should be the right of every American. It is essentially why the American Revolution was fought.

During his presidency, which included a violent assassination attempt, Reagan held to his stance, which essentially stated that the government's only role in firearm restrictions should be laws that punish the felonious use of guns, similar to the laws that punish the felonious use of vehicles. Regardless, in 2013 the governor of New York pushed through legislation aimed at removing the rights of firearm owners as part of a liberal progressive agenda. However the SAFE act only legislates those that are legal gun owners, and predictably for the first half of 2014, shootings rose 13% in New York City (Cavaliere, 2014).

Healthcare, which operated under the free-market system under Reagan, was completely overhauled in 2010 with the federalization of the healthcare system, commonly called Obamacare. Although the law was supposed to decrease the cost of health insurance through socializing the system, the truth was that premiums on average increased 49% from 2013 to 2014. The worst increase was a 271% hike in Missouri (Roy, 2014). Aside from the increases were promises to the citizenry that they could keep doctors and plans only to face waves of insurance collections in 2013 and 2014. Additionally, many who registered for the Affordable Care Act found they could not keep their doctors.

Under the latest administration two major governmental offices failed. At CPAC Reagan had defined the mission statement for the government: "Elected officials, their appointees, and government workers are expected to perform their public acts with honesty, openness, diligence, and special integrity." In 2010 the IRS began systematically targeting ultra-conservative groups by flagging their applications. This practice continued through 2012 when the issue was brought before the House Oversight Committee.

Additionally the Veterans Administration remains involved in a serious case of malpractice and fraud for falsifying data on the lengths of waits for VA doctors. Beginning in 2012, whistleblowers began to complain about long wait times for veterans. Several of the whistleblowers were transferred or place on administrative leave. Meanwhile the data system put in place to track wait times in 2013 was suspected of being manipulated. In fact it was alleged by Representative Jeff Miller that the lengthy wait times may have led to several veterans' deaths in Phoenix, Arizona.

4 JOIN OR DIE

Famously, Benjamin Franklin etched a cartoon depicting a snake cut into pieces as a means of illustrating the dangers of colonies taking a passive approach to the French and Indian War. The same cartoon received attention again during the Revolutionary War, much for the same reason. When Franklin stated: "we must all hang together, or assuredly we will hang separately," he understood that a majority was needed to succeed in pursuit of freedom (Franklin, 1919).

Reagan's closing remarks at CPAC included the following statement:

> Extreme taxation, excessive controls, oppressive government competition with business, galloping inflation, frustrated minorities and forgotten Americans are not the products of free enterprise. They are the residue of centralized bureaucracy, of government by a self-anointed elite.

Samuel Adams noted in August of 1776, that "Every art of corruption would be employed to loosen the bond of union which renders our resistance formidable." Newt Gingrich's Contract with America was the last noticeable coalition of Conservatives. Since then, "self-anointed elite" that Reagan was referring to has slowly dissolved the bond of Conservatives with a radical progressive ideology. What is worse is that there is self-anointed elite within the Republican Party doing as much damage to Conservatism as the Liberal Progressives. If the time has not already come to adjust the mission and goals of the Conservative ideology, it is certainly nearing a catastrophic failure of government that the Conservatives are not prepared to stop.

If we look to Jefferson and Reagan for leadership, then it is possible to create a platform to reinvigorate Conservatives. Before we can establish a full party platform it is important that we ensure a collective Conservative ideology is not temporary. While Reagan and Jefferson both understood that the Conservative belief system was the majority, both were aware that the ideology is split due to the party system. This split means that any Conservative majority is in fact a coalition. The only way that the coalition will stay strong is to recognize where the rifts are within Conservatism and to ensure that these differences are addressed prior to asserting a common platform.

We must:

- Break away from the elitist tendencies that have given the stigma of exclusivity that drives away voters, as well as quality candidates.
- We must hold ourselves to principles that guide the party, not principles that are arbitrarily established by

those seeking to alienate other Conservatives

- We must not be the anti- party. We must not run elections based off of simply not being the opposition candidate, we must run off of core principles and values. We must be the solution party.

- We must focus on the individual, not the party.

- We must compromise.

Once Conservatives accept that there are critical failure points within the coalition that have driven apart the majority and created deep divisions along party lines, only then can the ideology achieve a rebirth that will ensure the majority is successful in future elections. Unless the Conservative majority realizes these faults, the risk of a Progressive, Liberal mindset becoming the de facto rule of law in the United States. The state of American politics has finally come to the point where it is Join or Die.

With that in mind, the platform for the new Conservative movement needs to include the following planks in no particular order of importance:

1) Education

2) Foreign Policy

3) Military

4) Economy

5) Personal Choice and Freedoms

Contained within each of these planks are several points that are important to the overall success of America. TV and Radio personality Sean Hannity has often spoken of a need to identify key talking points for a successful campaign. While the new Conservative ideology will be too expansive for a campaign and talking points must be emphasized. It is not the time to talk just about problems; it is the time to address solutions.

5 EDUCATION PLANK

There is no greater importance of education than to ensure an intelligent electorate. This was the intention of both Jefferson and Reagan. Our public schools are not meeting the challenges of a modern society. Science, Technology, Engineering and Math jobs are among the fastest growing job market segment. There is a definitive lack of workers in the trades. In order to best ensure that these areas of education are addressed the following needs to occur:

- Repeal both the Common Core and No Child Left Behind legislation. Allow the best and the brightest students to excel, the country always needs future leaders, they should not be discouraged

- Encourage personal choice in education. Those students seeking out a trade should be allowed to attend high schools dedicated to the teaching of those trades. Those students who are interested and talented in STEM related coursework should have the opportunity to choose schools that best suit their needs.

- For all students, Newt Gingrich's plan makes use of a lot of the technology that already exists in schools, individualizing the materials and assignments to attempt to maximize a student's achievement and overall success (Gingrich, 2014). This is especially important for those students with learning disabilities and learning styles that are not compatible with typical chalk and talk.

- The classroom acts as an opportunity to teach core American values. Radicalizing the AP US History coursework to demonstrate how bad America acted in the past, as a means of pushing anti-government and anti-American behavior will only lead to an overall degradation of society.

- It is time to stop demonizing Proprietary Education. They provide education for the trades, often in areas that are overlooked by major universities. All universities should be subject to oversight by their state. While the federal government does oversee the accounting of their issuance of federal loans, this is where their influence on higher education must stop.

It is important for Conservatives to protect Education under the reserve powers clause. Education was never meant to be in the domain of Federal control. As both Reagan and Jefferson have pointed out, government works best when local control exists. Education should remain the domain of local governments, forcing all students to meet a federal standard is not what the founding fathers intended

for education.

6 FOREIGN POLICY PLANK

The government has systematically spent money to expand dominion and exert control in foreign nations. Jefferson made a point of avoiding entangling alliances during his inauguration, and Reagan pointed out that the government may need to rethink how America approaches foreign affairs.

- Reduce and eliminate foreign dependency on energy. At this point there is more than enough oil, and natural gas within the United States to become energy independent. Being energy independent will also allow the United States to play a larger role in international affairs without using the military.

- Related to reducing dependence on foreign energy, the Middle East situation was created by Britain and France. America has been forced to deal with this issue since World War I. If this requires a complete radicalization of thought pertaining to how we view the Middle East, then it may be time to sit down will the leaders from the Middle East, and allow them a chance to reshape the borders according to what makes sense. The only firm policies the United States should follow are: that under no circumstance will Israel be asked to turn over land, it should be made clear that any attempt to develop nuclear weapons will be met with force, and any attempt to train and encourage terrorism will be met with absolute force. The Middle East has a chance to make a change to suit their religious and economic needs, which should lessen the need for American involvement.

- Of the 9/11 terrorists at least three were here illegally. Immediately the United States needs to fix the immigration issue. Although the "hard" numbers are from 2012, the

Department of Homeland Security last estimated the number of illegal immigrants at 11.4 million. This is however before the 2013/2014 surge that saw tens of thousands of immigrants surge across a porous border. Border security is an immediate concern that impacts: economy, jobs, education and health. The new Conservative agenda should be centered on ensuring that the LEGAL immigration process is upheld, and that illegal immigration is stopped. A wall, guarded and enforced is a must to ensure the safety and security of American citizens. Current illegal immigrants must be issued a one year visa. This will allow a registration of all illegal immigrants, and provide them with an opportunity to apply for a legal immigration status or have one year to return to their country before deportation. Likewise expired visas need to be immediately enforced.

-War on Drugs. Although this well-intentioned attempt to stall or end the drug crisis in America, this effort costs billions of dollars every year, and has netted little in return.

What this has caused is actually a surge in cartels, a massive underground drug culture and prisons filled with drug-related criminals. Reagan had said that good governing allows for mistakes and corrections. It is time to move past this $1 trillion expenditure and to look for workable solutions. While many are not in favor of legalizing drug use, we must certainly expand treatment and recovery options, all of which must be turned back over to the states. While some of the illegal drug trade will be slowed with a secure border, like violent crime, drugs will never be able to be legislated out of existence.

7 MILITARY PLANK

Before discussing the current military Veterans must be addressed. America has a terrible track record for dealing with veterans. The VA needs to be completely overhauled. Veterans need to receive counselling and treatment for PTSD as part of standard procedure, regardless of whether they show overt signs of depression or mental illness.

Secondly, it is vitally important that US Military is made strong again. There has been a failure in support of the military since the start of the Vietnam War. Those in arms needs to be supported by the Government, and given the tools needed to succeed. As part of this issue the military needs to be used for the task for which it was designed. The American military was never meant to be a peacekeeping force in foreign lands. It was not meant to be used to help fight off diseases in other countries. The military is meant for one thing only – to protect America. Roosevelt summed up foreign diplomacy: "speak softly, and carry a big stick." The military needs to be returned to those standards, and understand that should they ever be asked to fight, they will have the full support, and financial commitment to win the war. Our military no longer should be bled needlessly.

Lastly, it is time for all of America to take an active role in public service and community involvement. While dismantling the militia may have made sense in an era when America's enemies were all on foreign shores, and consisted of large standing armies. However in the case of natural disasters and in the age of terrorism, those best equipped to deal with an immediate emergency would be the local militias, under local government control.

During the Revolution there were three distinct military organizations. Minutemen were local to an area, self- or locally outfitted and equipped and able to quickly respond to a crisis. While George Mason clearly defined what the enrollment was for the militia: "the militia, when properly formed, are in fact the people themselves…all men capable of bearing arms." Thomas Jefferson outlined the role of the militia: "A well-disciplined militia, our best reliance in peace and for the first moments of war till regulars may relieve them, I deem [one of] the essential principles of our Government, and consequently [one of] those which ought to shape its administration." The militia was often small in number, and local to the town in which they lived. State militia regiments that were uniformed and equipped as the official "regiments of the line." They were separate and distinct from the minutemen. Lastly there was a small Regular Army, responsible for protection of the United States.

In 1847, the local minuteman militias and state militia were essentially disbanded in favor of state only forces. The Militia act of 1903 furthered this agenda by creating a situation where the National Guard (formerly the State Militia forces) were defined in relation to the Regular Army in a much more homogenous way than ever before. The states were told how to arm, equip and train these troops, which could be called into federal service at any time. The last time a militia was used in official combat alongside state troops and the Regular army was in the pursuit of Pancho Villa prior to World War I. When Theodore Roosevelt was denied the right to establish a Volunteer regiment as allowed under the 1903 act, it became clear that the Federal Government was not going to permit any existence of military that they did not have direct control over.

It is time to reauthorize the unorganized militia as outlined in the Militia act of 1903. This would teach firearm safety and provide immediate emergency assistance in crisis situations. As a local volunteer organization, it would allow the Army and the National Guard to be used only as they were intended. This would allow for a more economical approach to emergencies within US borders. It would allow for situations to be handled on a local level. If necessary, the National Guard could be called up to step into a situation that the local government could not handle on its own.

8 ECONOMY PLANK

The liberal progressive movement that created a socialist society has stigmatized Conservatives as Capitalists. While the Republican Party had grown to be associated with big-business there has to be a realization that this is not the goal of the new Conservative. The free-market system, whereby people have a right to work, is what will revitalize the American economy. The response from the radicalized progressives has been to portray Conservatives as racist and exclusionary. Regardless of race or ethnicity, it has to be through recognizing that keeping a class of people constantly poor does nothing to aide our economic woes. Raising the minimum wage to $15 an hour will only serve to keep people in minimum wage jobs, as they will be comfortable enough not to seek out advancement. Conservatives believe that all men and women are created equal, that they should strive to work, strive to produce, and strive to contribute.

Conservatives realize that to address our economic issues, to balance our budget and repay our national debt, but it cannot happen without a fully functional American workforce. This is why there is an appeal to reduce the government entitlement programs and create jobs. When the liberal agenda cannot convince people of a racial or economic threat they have resorted to attacking industries on short-sighted and often incorrect data. Using false science we were deceived into fear of a global warming trend that has not happened. As a result timber and energy industries that should be employing thousands of Americans are held hostage. Today North Dakota and Texas are experiencing growth in employment. Alaska should be leading the nation in energy production, except for misguided governmental interference.

In order to help fix the economic crisis Conservatives must:

- Sharply decrease entitlement programs
- Seek out initiatives to assist in getting people back to work. This will be aided by ensuring that energy production is increased within the United States
- Switch to a flat tax.
- Give tax breaks to encourage the development and success of small businesses
- Give tax incentives to businesses that are US based, and incentives to those businesses that submit plans to return to the United States.
- Seek out wasteful government spending and eliminate those departments.
- Adopt the Penny Plan. This plan promises to cut one

penny of every tax dollar spent. The longer that Big Government spending continues, the longer that the penny plan must remain in practice.

It is essential as Conservatives that we must constantly reinforce an understanding that governmental spending will not result in better lives, governmental spending results in governmental intrusion into our daily lives.

9 PERSONAL CHOICE PLANK

Personal freedoms and personal choice is a complicated discussion for Conservatives. Part of the issue with uniting the Conservative majority is the elitist attitude that many Conservatives use when discussing personal choice.

Alexander Hamilton in April of 1798 stated that as a goal of the French Revolution, "equal pains have been taken to deprave the morals as to extinguish the religion of a country, if indeed morality in a community can be separated from religion." The founding fathers were well aware that a country could not be run as religion, so that a religious leader would never force an ideology on a whole nation, and indoctrinate a holy war. However the founding fathers were equally aware that religion was a central part of establishing the moral compass of any country. What the founding fathers did not do was establish who was more right in the religious debate, to the founders it did not matter what religion a person practiced.

To ensure that no religion would ever assume total control, the 1st Amendment prohibited the adoption of a national religion. This has long been misinterpreted as a ban on religion; the amendment and the establishment clause are in reality a continuation of the principle that government is to remain neutral on matters of religion. It does not state that anyone should lock away beliefs in a closet, or to only to practice beliefs where no one else can see them. The founders realized that religions teach tolerance, acceptance and help to define what is right and what is wrong.

To ensure that the message of personal choice is accurately conveyed the idea of there being a superior religion, or that one's religious beliefs are in some was superior to another is not conducive to collaboration. Reagan stated at CPAC: "Our candidates must be willing to communicate with every level of society, because the principles we espouse are universal and cut across traditional lines."

To ensure that Conservatives are united, the principles should be simple:

- Family
- Faith
- Values and Ethics

These are not class or ethnicity related. Strong families and faith allow for a moral compass which should guide the nation. The statistics for crime and drug use in single parent households are devastating. When at all possible Conservatives should talk about the benefits of family and religion, keeping in mind Reagan's principle that the individual is important. What the elite in the party deem as the best religion is not as important as the individual's choice to adopt and follow a religion in the manner in which they choose. Simply by understanding that rights do not come from a government that person has accepted some of the core Conservative philosophy and they should not be turned away.

10 CONCLUSION

Reagan left office in 1980, and no one president has yet to repeat his vision. While Newt Gingrich was able to enact Reagan style reforms, once out of office, there was no clear Conservative voice in government, and yet Conservatism is still the majority ideology in the United States. As of 2011, 40% of Americans considered themselves Conservative, 35% Moderate and only 21% Liberal. The smallest gap between Conservative ideology and Liberal ideology was in 2007 when Liberals only ranked below Conservatives by 15 points (Gallup, 2012). While Conservatives remain a majority in number they are in danger of letting a vocal, active minority dominating the political, social and economic culture of America.

Americans have been conditioned to accept that the government is an arbitrator of rights. Education has been federalized with some disastrous results. Debt spending and entitlement programs have incentivized a defeatist lifestyle supported by tax dollars. Faith, heritage and beliefs are all regarded as sources of embarrassment, guilt or ridicule. Students should not be suspended for saying "Bless You," nor should there be a ban on voluntary school prayer, regardless of what religion the students are that are praying. The radical movement that allows for a ban of American Flags on American soil is meant to disrupt and strip away the values and beliefs that are the very fabric of an American identity. Once again Conservatives are called on to join against the tyranny of a small coalition of radicals or watch passively as America dies. It is time to reinforce the unalienable right of personal choice. As Conservatives we are 40% of the population.

Our task now is not to sell a philosophy, but to make the majority of Americans, who already share that philosophy, see that modern conservatism offers them a political home. We are not a cult; we are members of a majority. Let's act and talk like it. ~ Ronald Reagan at CPAC

Bibliography

Berry, S. (2014, July 12). *COMMON CORE ARCHITECT DAVID COLEMAN'S NEXT DECEPTION: THE NEW AP U.S. HISTORY EXAM*. Retrieved from Breitbart News: http://www.breitbart.com/Big-Government/2014/07/11/David-Coleman-s-Second-Deception-After-Common-Core-The-New-AP-U-S-History-Exam

Bidwell, A. (2013, August 6). Half of Outstanding Student Loan Debt Isn't Being Repaid. *US News and World Report*.

Biery, M. A. (2014, Feb 2). *Private-Company Growth Slowed In 2013*. Retrieved from Forbes: http://www.forbes.com/sites/sageworks/2014/02/02/private-company-growth-slowed-in-2013/

Cavaliere, V. (2014, June 10). *Even as shootings rise, murder rate falls in New York City*. Retrieved from Reuters: http://www.reuters.com/article/2014/06/10/us-usa-newyork-crime-idUSKBN0EL27520140610

Chantrill, C. (2014). *US Entitlement Spending Growth*. Retrieved from US Government Spending: http://www.usgovernmentspending.com/entitlement_spending

Ellis, J. J. (1998). *American Sphinx: The Character of Thomas Jefferson*. New York: Vintage.

Franklin, B. (1919, July 4). Quotation. In J. Bartlett, *Familiar Quotations* (10 ed.). Blue Ribbon Books.

Gallup . (2012, January 12). *Conservatives Remain the Largest Ideological Group in U.S.* Retrieved 2014, from Gallup Politics: http://www.gallup.com/poll/152021/conservatives-remain-largest-ideological-group.aspx

Gingrich, N. (2014, August 1). *Get schools out of the 1890s.* Retrieved from CNN: http://www.cnn.com/2014/08/01/opinion/gingrich-schools-blended-teaching-technology/

Hamilton, A. (1788). 84. In A. M. Hamliton, *Federalist Papers.* New York: J. and A. McLean.

Hamilton, J. C. (1851). *The Works of Alexander Hamilton.* New York: John F. Trow.

Jefferson, T. (1801, March 4). *Thomas Jefferson First Inaugural Address.* Retrieved from Avalon Project at Yale Law School: http://avalon.law.yale.edu/19th_century/jefinau1.asp

Lambert, F. (2003). *The Founding Fathers and the Place of Religion in America.* Princeton, NJ: Princeton University Press.

Leip, D. (2012). *1980 Presidential General Election Results.* Retrieved from US Election Atlas: http://uselectionatlas.org/RESULTS/

Mason, G. (1788). *Debates in Virginia Convention on Ratification of the Constitution.* Richmond.

Ritz, E. (2013, October 23). *Mike Rowe on How Many Are Following the 'Worst Advice in the History of the World'.* Retrieved from The Blaze: http://www.theblaze.com/stories/2013/10/23/mike-rowe-of-dirty-jobs-speaks-about-hard-work-how-many-are-following-the-worst-advice-in-the-history-of-the-world/#

Roy, A. (2014, June 18). *3,137-County Analysis: Obamacare Increased 2014 Individual-Market Premiums By Average Of 49%.* Retrieved from Forbes: http://www.forbes.com/sites/theapothecary/2014/06/18/3137-county-analysis-obamacare-increased-2014-individual-market-premiums-by-average-of-49/

Stilwell, V. (2014, May 2). *Workforce Participation at 36-Year Low as Jobs Climb.* Retrieved from Bloomberg:

http://www.bloomberg.com/news/2014-05-02/workforce-participation-at-36-year-low-even-as-more-jobs-beckon.html

Turley, J. (2011, September 29). *Obama: A disaster for civil liberties.* Retrieved from Los Angeles Times: http://articles.latimes.com/2011/sep/29/opinion/la-oe-turley-civil-liberties-20110929

USDA. (2014, September 5). *Supplemental Nutrition Assistance Program.* Retrieved from Food and Nutrition Service: http://www.fns.usda.gov/sites/default/files/pd/SNAPsummary.pdf

World Bank. (2014, September 19). *GDP Growth Rate.* Retrieved from Public Data: https://www.google.com/publicdata/explore?ds=d5bncppjof8f9_&met_y=ny_gdp_mktp_kd_zg&idim=country:USA:IND:GBR&hl=en&dl=en

CHRIS SCHNUPP

ABOUT THE AUTHOR

Chris Schnupp holds degrees in history and law. He is the author of *The Long Island Company: A History of Company H, 1st Regiment of US Sharpshooters*

www.ingramcontent.com/pod-product-compliance
Lightning Source LLC
Chambersburg PA
CBHW070606290526
45790CB00002B/800